wordstoremember

this journal belongs to:

_____

I want to be a tiger next week.

introduction

We dutifully record our children's footprints, monthly pounds and ounces, and first steps in the baby books. We video their birthday parties, school shows, and pre-Olympic sporting events. We've got albums/boxes/rooms full of photographs, not to mention all the digital snapshots we keep meaning to organize . . . tomorrow.

But what about all the wonderful things our children *say*?

Hardly a day goes by without one of them saying something funny, or sweet, or poignant, or interestingly odd, or straight-out brilliant, right? In the moment we are sure we will always remember this fabulous utterance, only to find a day (or sixty seconds) later it has completely vanished from our brain. Or we say, "I've got to write that down!" and we really mean to, but then, you know . . .

The mom part of me is all-too-familiar with this kind of distraction, ten things going on at once. Yet the writer part of me is somehow always paying attention to words. The convergence of those two realities led to the book in your hands. When my children were small, I managed to collect many of their "spoken gems." Some of the quotes sprinkled throughout the following pages are courtesy of my kids—Justin, Miles, and Paris—and are definitely the inspiration for this new kind of journal, a sort of "verbal album."

Even more than photographs, looking through our family's quote books is still my—and my kids'—absolute favorite way to reminisce, laugh, and reflect. I hope in turn that this specialized journal will serve as a convenient and lasting home for your children's amusing musings. May it be a source of pleasure for years to come.

Amy

I think yellow taxicabs are actually baby school buses.

I'm going to make sure the trees are tall enough in the morning.

When the baby comes she'll learn
to walk and live somewhere else.

Dreams are so you don't get lonesome when you're sleeping.

When I learn to drive, I'm going to drive to the park every day to play.

clementines

Who named all the foods?

Here's what you need to know about kids, Mom:
Basically, they want to stay up late,
eat candy, and not read.

Do you think there are more people in the world than inches in the sea?

Mom, why did you make me the little brother?

Those aren't stars, silly. They're sprinkles!

You can be sad, but not cry.

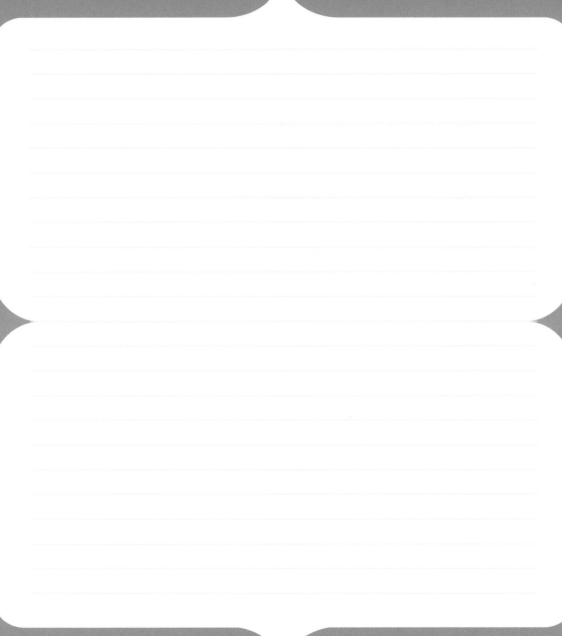

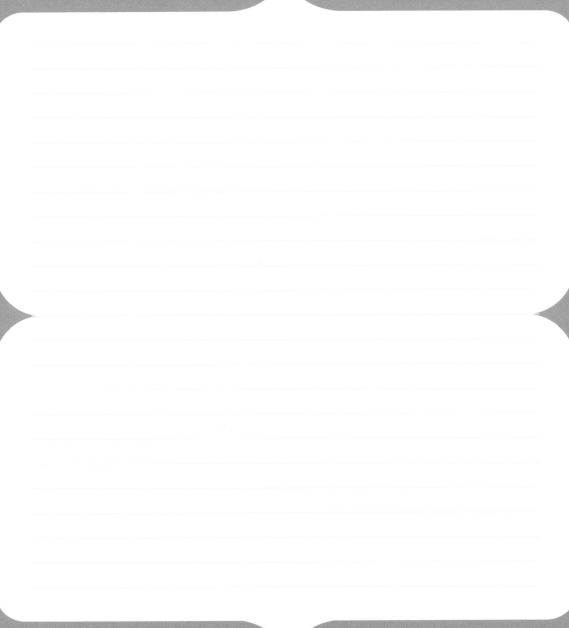

Where is the mailbox to heaven?

Mommy, I can't breathe out of my right ostrich.

Isn't it so cool how I was born on the same day as my birthday?

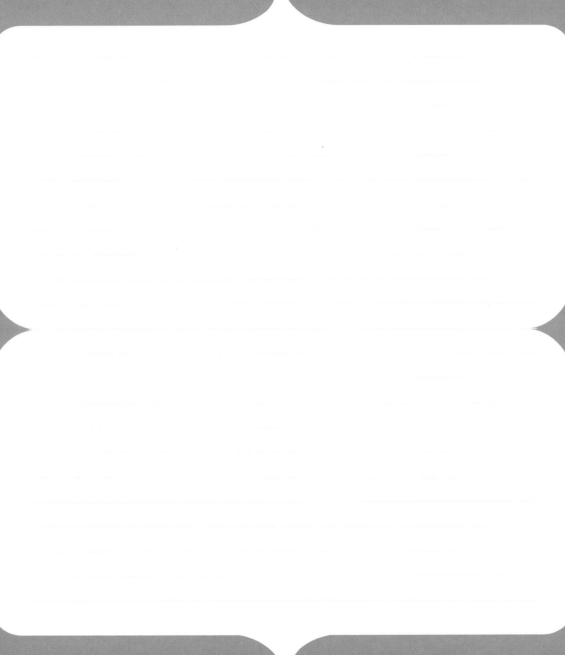

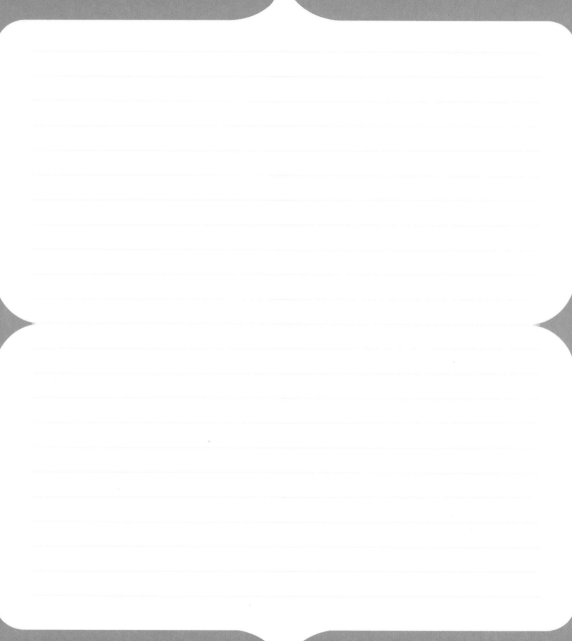

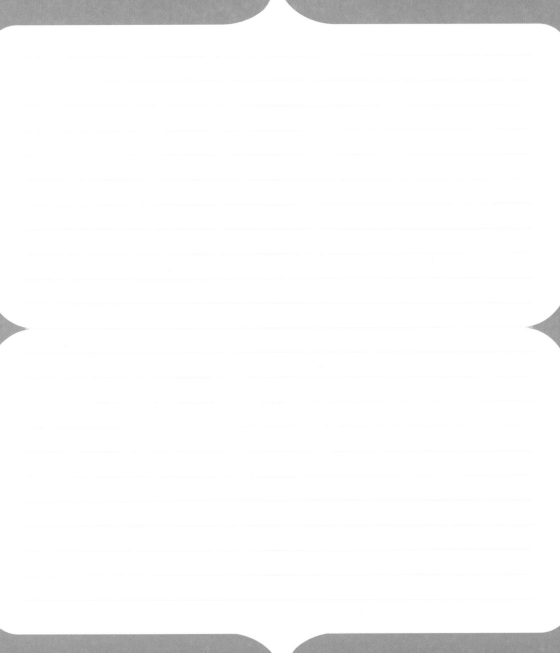

I don't want to wear a button-down shirt to school.
I don't want the girls admiring me.

Gum is my favorite sport.

When we're sleeping, we're just wasting time, we could be playing.

A good dad carries you from the car into the house when you're tired.

acknowledgments

Quotes from a Cast of Excellent Young Friends*

Ella Berry, Chicago, IL
- When the baby comes she'll learn to walk and live somewhere else.

Lana Berry, Chicago, IL
- Mommy, I can't breathe out of my right ostrich.

Ivy Harper, Mamaroneck, NY
- When I learn to drive I'm going to drive to the park everyday to play.

Matt Kaufmann, Highland Park, IL
- I don't want to wear a button-down shirt to school. I don't want the girls admiring me.

Andy Kaufmann, Highland Park, IL
- Mom, why did you make me the little brother?

Tyler Froelich, Highland Park, IL
- Where is the mailbox to heaven?

Justin Rosenthal, Chicago, IL
- I'm going to make sure the trees are tall enough in the morning.
- Here's what you need to know about kids, Mom: Basically, they want to stay up late, eat candy, and not read.

- Do you think there are more people in the world than inches in the sea?
- You can be sad but not cry.
- When we're sleeping, we're just wasting time, we could be playing.

Miles Rosenthal, Chicago, IL
- I think yellow taxicabs are actually baby school buses.
- Dreams are so you don't get lonesome when you're sleeping.
- Who named all the foods?
- I'm always thinking of something. And when I'm not thinking of something, I'm writing words in cursive in my head.

Paris Rosenthal, Chicago, IL
- Those aren't stars, silly. They're sprinkles!
- Isn't it so cool how I was born on the same day as my birthday?
- Gum is my favorite sport.
- A good dad carries you from the car into the house when you're tired.

* As some of the cast members are now actually teenagers (gasp), it should be noted that all quotes were in fact spoken when the children were "little."

A special thank you to all the mamas:

Ava Berry, Charise Mericle Harper, Beth Kaufmann,
and Katie Froelich.

About the Author

Amy Krouse Rosenthal is the author of the memoir
Encyclopedia of an Ordinary Life, and of several books
for children, including *Little Pea*, *The OK Book*, and
Cookies: Bite-Size Life Lessons. For a complete listing of
the other journals and gift products in her Amy K. line—
including *The Belly Book*, *Your Birthday Book*, and *Karma
Checks*—please visit www.potterstyle.com.

About the Artist

Ida Pearle was born and raised and currently lives in
New York City. She was educated at the United Nations
International School, La Guardia High School of the Arts,
and the Cooper Union for Advancement of Science and
Art. Ida creates cut-paper collages for album covers,
custom-order invitations, and prints for nursery walls.
Visit her at www.idapearle.com.

Potter Style

Text copyright © 2008 by
Amy Krouse Rosenthal

Illustrations copyright © 2008 by
Ida Pearle

Published in the United States by Clarkson
Potter/Publishers, an imprint of the Crown
Publishing Group, a division of Random House,
Inc., New York.

Potter Style is a trademark and Potter and
colophon are registered trademarks of Random
House, Inc.

Design by Jennifer K. Beal

Printed in China
ISBN: 978-0-307-39571-9

10 9 8 7 6 5 4 3 2

First Edition